OMG! YOU THINK
I'M FAT!?!

How to talk (or NOT talk)
about your child's weight

Madeleine Berg, MS, RD, CDN

Dear Rica,

Healthy regards,

Madeleine Berg

Cover design by Jacob Berg

FIRST EDITION

OMG! You Think I'm Fat!?!
How to talk (or NOT talk) about your child's weight

Library of Congress Control Number: 2018915308

ISBN: 978-0-578-43954-9

For all the mothers and daughters who have trusted me with their stories.

TV Dinner
By Nancy Greene

Fantasy mother.
Home from school, I run to you,
my comfort food.
Warm mashed potatoes.
Pillows of layer-cake lap.

Mop up each confession.
Power players purging and
letting go of perfect.
Snuggle up and strengthen.
Ugly-cry surrender.

Bring on the cotton candy.
Gather round the jet plane.
Hips sway with John Travolta.
Smooth, cool ice cream sundae.
The taste of letting joy in.

Show me now your gristle.
Parade around your damage.
Red radio flyer wagon.
Calvin Klein size tens waltz through
girls' leadership academy.

Table of Contents

INTRODUCTION:

Why this book is for you

The car door slams. She still can hear her mother yelling.

"I'm telling you this for your own good! You'll never find a boyfriend if you keep gaining weight."

The girl's cheeks are burning. She didn't mean to eat all those cookies. They weren't even that good. She knows her mother is right. She is unlovable.

Change a few details and this is your story. You are that mother, that daughter. The mother's intentions are not bad. The daughter probably *would* be better off if she lost a few pounds. But should her mother be telling her that?

I'm not an advocate of the "Health at Every Size" or "Fat Acceptance" movements. I know how concerning it is to watch your child's weight escalate. Childhood obesity is linked to depression, anxiety, and a myriad of other health problems. Even a modest unwanted increase in weight can cause a child to become self-conscious and have lower self-esteem. Much has been written about the childhood obesity epidemic, yet the fact that all our "helping" is making the problem worse has been largely ignored. What we've tried so far isn't working. You know this is true, or you wouldn't be reading this. This book is for good, caring parents such as yourself, who are ready to try a new approach.

By the time most parents look for help, the relationship between parent and child regarding weight and food has already started to turn toxic. Even adult children are not immune from the hurt caused by their parent tossing off a casual comment or disapproving glance. There is no statute of limitations on the damage caused by parents trying to control their child's weight. Weight and weight control are hot button issues for many of us throughout our lives. I'm not saying I have all the answers, but I can say with absolute certainty that trying to control your child's weight is like trying to catch a knife in midair. Not only is it impossible, but any attempt you make will only cause more damage.

Why should you take my word for it? My credentials establish me as a nutrition expert. I have been a registered dietitian nutritionist for three decades with nutrition degrees from Cornell University and New York University. But it's not my credentials that compelled me to write this book. This is the book I wish my mother had read. This is my story as much as it is yours. It is a story of hope and change and healing. As the mother of four boys with a full-time nutrition practice on Long Island, I have no time or patience for busy work. This book is filled with practical suggestions and advice based on real-life experiences. I have collected hundreds of stories from clients, friends, and family to form this book, to tell our story.

This book is for you if ...

- You're always looking out for your child's best interest.
- You've tried everything else.
- You're worried your child is getting fat.
- Your pediatrician already told you your child is overweight or obese.
- You were raised by the food police.
- You fear you are becoming the food police.
- You dread the mealtime battles.
- You don't want to pass eating issues on to your kids.

- You're ready to break the diet cycle.
- You've ever said, "Does this dress make me look fat?"
- You think what you say is "not that bad."
- You think your child can handle your comments.

I know you want what is best for your child. There is no quick fix or miracle cure. Your child may always struggle to maintain a healthy weight. You may always struggle to come to terms with your child's weight. You may always struggle to come to terms with your own weight. The purpose of this book is to let you know you are not alone. It is intended to help shed light on the problem, identify the behaviors that are not working, and help create a positive, constructive path for you and your child to move forward.

CHAPTER 1:

How did we get here?

My grandmother, who came to this country as a refugee from Europe 100 years ago, viewed fat people as lazy, unattractive, and lacking discipline. A century later, these stereotypes persist. Our negative biases are passed down from generation to generation.

The familial dysfunction surrounding weight and weight control started long before childhood obesity was declared an epidemic in this country. Currently, there are more people in the United States that are overweight or obese than there are people of normal weight. Even though a majority of the country is considered "fat," overweight people are still discriminated against in the workplace, the dating pool, the medical community, the fashion industry, and at home.

We live in an obesogenic society. Everything about how we live today is designed to make us overweight. A 2015 study found that if you're American and you're awake, you're eating. We are awake an average of fifteen hours a day, and we are constantly eating. Living in America is like one giant all you can eat buffet. You can drive up to a fast food restaurant, roll down your window, give the cashier one dollar and drive away with 500 calories. Value meals that combine a burger, fries and a drink have become the default option. It takes a lot of effort *not* to be overweight in this country. Even the diet industry is designed to make us overweight by selling shakes, bars, packaged meals, snacks and supplements that promise a quick fix, but often lead to even more weight gain. A vicious cycle ensues; one that is lucrative for the diet industry, but devastating to our waistlines.

Whichever side of the tracks you live on, rich or poor, there is guaranteed to be a fast food restaurant nearby. In the past, the health effects of eating too much fast food were mainly a concern in disadvantaged communities, where healthier, affordable options were not available. Not anymore. Now, the socioeconomic disparity in obesity has almost disappeared and is evenly distributed across economic lines. Today the average American eats about four or five commercially prepared meals per week. Every time you eat out or bring food in, you're getting more calories than you would if you had a home cooked meal. Since the 1970's the average size of a fast food meal has increased by a staggering 138%. Countless parents have come to me desperate for help because their child is gaining weight. When I suggest more home cooked meals, the typical response is, "That's not going to happen. What else can I do??"

We are eating more and moving less. Even avid exercisers find themselves sitting an average of thirteen hours a day. I'm sitting right now and you most likely are too. Our children only spend half as much time as we did playing outside. Instead of spending hours playing tag, hide and seek or kickball, today's children are inside gaming. It used to be taken for granted that a child would walk or ride their bike to a friend's house. Now parents are much more protective. Children are discouraged from using active transportation like walking or bike riding. Even if a child spends some time running around outside, it's not enough to offset the rest of the day spent sitting and eating snacks.

Children are more overweight now than at any time in history. A 2016 study showed one in five children is obese. The obesogenic society we've created needs to be addressed, but that is not the focus of this book. I'm not a policy expert. I am an expert on how a parent's beliefs and attitudes towards their child's weight are compounding an already unmanageable problem. Add to the mix our current methods of weight control, which are ineffective and border on the barbaric, and you have a toxic mess.

It's natural for parents to want their children to have every advantage in life and being overweight is a distinct disadvantage. Here's the conundrum: research shows that when a child thinks their parent thinks they're overweight, they are more likely to become overweight--even if they weren't to begin with. Trying to get out in front of the problem can create the problem. Fast food, video games, and supersize portions are all obvious culprits in the current childhood obesity crisis. But concerned parents? I bet you didn't see that coming. Unless of course, you were raised by a parent who was trying to keep you from getting fat. If that's the case you know exactly what I mean.

Parents like Julie, who herself was subject to weight control methods by her parents, are often the worst offenders. Julie can recall in vivid detail how her mom forced her to exercise, monitored her calorie intake, and constantly made snide comments about her weight. Now a mom of two daughters herself, Julie is struggling not to make the same mistakes. On the one hand, she acknowledges how terrible her mom made her feel. On the other hand, she really, really doesn't want her own daughters to grow up overweight.

By all accounts, Julie is a very caring, concerned mom, yet she is perpetuating a very unhealthy dynamic. Her justification is her intense concern for her children's health. She is self-aware enough to know she is repeating her mother's hurtful pattern, but a part of her still thinks her actions are justified. One of the hardest things for parents to do is step back, especially when the stakes are so high.

It's not hard to see how we got here. Our attitude towards people who are overweight has not changed much in the past 100 years. Everything about how we live now almost guarantees our kids will be overweight, including the diet industry. Caring parents who try to step in and help are only making the problem worse.

CHAPTER 2:

I can't just do nothing

I hear your frustration: "I can't just do nothing! If I don't do *something* my child will continue to gain weight." Before you "do" anything, please understand the dangers.

In all my years of practice, I have had exactly one client say, "I'm so glad my mother put me on a diet." Usually, I hear a catalog of grievances. Lisa's mom made her bring fish for lunch in elementary school every day. Helene was put on a diet to fit into her Holy Communion dress, her sweet-sixteen dress, her prom dress, and her wedding dress because, you know, you don't want to look fat in the pictures. Cami's brothers got ice cream, but she was only allowed orange sherbet. Shelly's dad pinched the fat on her belly, back, and chin. When Todd was in middle school, he was dragged to Weight Watchers meetings with his mom and all the other ladies in town. Gabi wasn't allowed pizza at birthday parties. Sandy's dad called her a chunky monkey as she was getting ready to go on a date. Lori's sister was the skinny one, and Lori was the other one. Stephanie's mom paid her to lose weight. Anna's dad showed up with a fistful of hundred-dollar bills over Christmas to hire her a personal trainer. The list goes on.

The collective culture helps shape our views about what is considered attractive and which body types are most desirable. The effect of the media, and especially social media, has on our attitudes towards body weight and body image has been well established. Media takes a lot of heat for putting unreasonable pressure on children to look a certain way. It's undeniable that media adds fuel to the fire, but it cannot entirely be blamed for lighting the match. The fire starts much closer to home. Our parents' body image and their relationship with food start shaping ours almost from birth. We like to blame everything on the mother, but a dad's attitudes can be equally damaging. Add concerned grandparents and maybe an aunt or uncle to the mix and our children get the message loud and clear: Your self-worth is tied to how much you weigh.

Every time you look in the mirror and declare how fat you are or how much you hate your body, you're teaching your child to hate theirs. Every weight loss diet you go on that requires you to eat differently than your family, teaches your child not to trust food. Your dissatisfaction with your body and your relationship with food is passed down to your children. Just like it was passed down to you. Hating your body doesn't have to be part of your family's legacy. It is possible for your children to have a healthy relationship with food and a positive body image even if yours is less than ideal.

Whether you struggle with your weight, or not, your attitudes about weight are known to your children. If you're not convinced, take a minute to ask them. Their answers will be revealing. Children absorb everything we do and say. The moment you notice your child is starting to put on extra weight, they notice you noticing. A look can be as powerful as words. You know that look your mother gave you when she thought you were eating too much? What effect did it have on you? Did you want to stop eating, or did you want to eat more? Did those silent reprimands leave you with positive or negative feelings?

As smart as you are, your children are even smarter. They see right through your attempts to control their eating.

"What if I focus on her being healthy and not on her weight?"

"What if I just educate her on good choices and bad choices? Maybe she doesn't realize that eating a sleeve of cookies is too much."

"What if it comes from her dad or grandma? After all, I can't control what they say."

"What if I use my dying breath, like Cindy's mom did, to let her know she really should lose some weight?"

"What if I bring her to you and you tell her?"

All this parental intervention will most definitely fail to "nip it in the bud." Sherri, the only girl who was grateful to her Mom for putting her on a diet, went on to develop an eating disorder that has followed her into adulthood. Even more disturbing, Sherri's son is struggling with the same issues. When her son, Andrew, was just eight years old he told her, "I can't wait until I grow up and have my own money so I can buy as many chocolate chip cookies as I want, and you can't tell me I've had enough." Sherri knows she is repeating the same unhealthy pattern from her childhood and yet she feels justified to send Andrew, now a teenager, to Weight Watchers. She is passing her twisted relationship with food and body image down to her son.

Every one of these children grew up to be an adult struggling with weight and feelings of weight-related shame. Even as they grew up, got married, had kids of their own and successful careers, feelings of inadequacy lurked beneath the surface. You're thinking, your comments aren't that bad. That your child is an exception. That your child is mature enough to handle it. Please listen to me when I say that, when it comes to weight and body image, it doesn't take much for negative feelings to take root.

I ran into my neighbor Andrea the other day and I asked how her son, Michael, was doing in college. She said, "You know how his weight fluctuates, so I told him he better not come home from college fat." Then she laughed. She rushed in to explain, that it's OK that she ribs Michael about his weight because she keeps cookies in the house, not like how she grew up. It's never OK to make fun of your child's weight, even if it seems they are in on the joke.

The philosophy of intuitive eating relies on listening to your own body's signals for hunger and fullness. According to Allison Tannenbaum, MS, RDN, a specialist in pediatric nutrition and feeding, the feeding dilemma starts at birth and surfaces again at six months when parents generally start introducing solid foods. Babies have an innate ability to self-regulate their intake. When parents try to circumvent this, they lay the groundwork for lifelong eating problems. It can be nerve-racking to trust that your baby is getting enough calories without you urging them to eat more. The best outcomes happen when babies lead the way when it comes to if and how much they want to eat.

If you're like most parents, you have no idea you are approaching feeding wrong, and it may not become obvious until your children get older. When you micromanage what and how much they are eating, you are robbing them of the opportunity to develop their sense of hunger and fullness. Telling your child, they have eaten too much or too little is the exact opposite of intuitive eating.

It's anxiety producing for parents to give up mealtime control. It makes no difference if your child is a picky eater or has an insatiable appetite. Taking a step back during mealtime and trusting your child's instincts seems to be nearly impossible for parents to do. It gets even trickier if one of your children is on the high end of the growth chart and the other is failing to thrive.

My four boys are very close in age. For much of their childhood, I was the only adult in the house. It's safe to say I was outnumbered. I cooked them dinner every night but they didn't always eat it. Some nights three out of the four ate, sometimes only two. My clients were appalled when I would tell them, "Seventy-five percent of my kids ate dinner tonight. I think that's pretty good." Like all kids, my children's tastes grew and changed, and changed again. My son Ari went through a phase where he would only eat nuts and berries. Not surprisingly, he is now a vegetarian. It's the parent's job to provide the food and the child's job to decide how much they are going to eat if anything at all. My attitude when my children were growing up was always, "Eat or don't eat, but I did my job by cooking dinner."

We have all made mistakes. Who in this country hasn't held dessert for the ransom of a clean plate? Seriously, how else will children eat their vegetables? Believe it or not, children will be just fine if they skip a few veggies. Bribing them with food is the bigger problem. I just saw the cutest home video of a preschooler eating a big dish of ice cream as a reward for not biting his friend at school that day. It was so cute, it went viral. I'm not saying food rewards don't work in the short term, I'm saying they contribute to an unhealthy relationship with food later.

Obesity runs in families, yet it is common for one sibling to tend to gain weight and the other to be more naturally lean. I often hear, "She is built like her dad, but unfortunately her sister is built like me." How is a child supposed to handle that? Children have a heightened sense of awareness when it comes to fairness. Their senses are particularly honed when it comes to how they are being treated compared to their siblings. Parents feel justified to feed a lean picky eater anything they want, while they restrict the more robust child to mainly healthy choices. This is unfair. The only thing this strategy creates is bad feelings and bad habits. Your picky eater will not starve if you don't cater to their every food whim, and the world will not end if your chubby child eats ice cream.

Sue, a working mom with four children, is always pressed for time and yet she still manages to drive all over town to pick up food for her picky eater. This has not gone unnoticed by her other children. Bria, who is overweight, has noticed that her mom goes out of her way to accommodate her sister Angela's food preferences. Bria, on the other hand, is told to prepare her own healthy low-calorie meals and to do calisthenics in her room. Sue is a very loving and involved mom. She grew up with a mom who was critical of her weight, so she knows the lasting damage it can cause. She is trying not to repeat the same pattern from her own childhood. Food and weight are her blind spots. These issues prove to be too emotionally charged, and Sue feels compelled to intervene. The destructive, dysfunctional pattern continues.

Rachel is the mother of twin teenage girls, Tara and Emily. Tara is completely disinterested in eating and Emily seems to have an insatiable appetite. Rachel's story is a typical one. She was a dancer and grew up with a mom who controlled her calorie intake. When she went to college, the floodgates opened and Rachel gained fifty pounds. Today Rachel's weight is normal but her attitudes about the importance of weight, food, and exercise are distorted. Her daughter Emily is paying the price. When I first met Emily, she was thirteen years old and about ten pounds overweight. By the time she came to me, she had already been to several specialists to determine if her weight gain was caused by a hormonal imbalance or if there was another medical explanation. All her test results were within normal limits.

Emily is an exceptionally good child and wants to make her mom happy. She has tried to control her appetite by eating low carb, gluten-free, low sugar, high protein, keto, Paleo. The list goes on and on. In the beginning, I naively thought I could inspire Emily to catch the fitness bug. I assured her mom, like I assured many other moms, that I would deliver the same "healthy eating, exercise is fun" message they tried to deliver but that it would be better received coming from a professional. That was before I realized the damage that can be done just by taking your child to a nutritionist. It was this family that caused me to rethink my entire approach to working with children. While I'm willing to work with parents, I no longer treat children in my office unless they are old enough to drive to me on their own.

Eventually, every meeting I had with Emily and Rachel would end the same way. I would implore Rachel to back off and she would respond that Emily would just keep gaining weight if they didn't do something. Emily, heartbreakingly, would vow to be good and to try even harder. Emily just left for college to study psychology. I'm rooting for her. Being away at college may finally give Emily the strength to stop living her mother's narrative and start living her own. My hope is that when Emily has a family of her own she will stop this cycle from repeating.

I am not asking you to do nothing. There are some things you can do.

- Allow your child to develop their own sense of hunger and fullness.
- Treat your children fairly.
- Be a positive role model.
- Don't reward your children for eating or use food as a reward to shape behavior.

CHAPTER 3:

According to our charts, your child is obese

Pediatricians are tasked with screening children for obesity during annual well-child visits. If a child is found to have a BMI greater or equal than the 85th percentile for height and weight they are considered overweight, a BMI above 95th percentile is considered obese. According to The American Academy of Pediatrics Policy Statement, pediatricians should talk to parents in a nonjudgmental, blame-free manner. Ideally, interventions should begin as soon as a problem or potential problem is detected. The Academy also warns against the detrimental effects of over-controlling parental behavior.

On the surface, these recommendations sound reasonable and prudent. The parents and child are alerted as soon as a child's BMI is flagged as overweight. The child is told to limit fast food and sugary snacks, engage in physical activity for at least twenty minutes a day and limit nonacademic screen time to one to two hours per day. Problem solved! As if it were so simple. The harsh reality is that pediatric obesity screening and the subsequent interventions rarely have the intended effect.

Consider your child's point of view. It is mortifying to be told you are fat. Using the clinical term obesity does not soften the blow. As your child is listening to the doctor tell them they can't have fast food or soda anymore and that they must limit their favorite video game, how can they not feel punished? They start to wonder why these new rules only apply to them and not their siblings. What are they supposed to do at a birthday party or when hanging out with friends? From the moment your child is flagged as obese, visits to the doctor become lifelong traumatic events. Haile, a beautiful young woman in my practice, breaks out in hives to this day every time she goes to the doctor because she was so traumatized as an overweight child.

It's not just traumatic for the child. Parents feel under attack too. Even the most tactful, in-tune pediatrician has a difficult time projecting a nonjudgmental, blame-free manner while talking to parents about their child's weight. As the parent, you feel blamed. You are being blamed. You buy the food, you make the rules, you are supposed to encourage physical activity. How can you not feel responsible? If you are doing so many things wrong, how is it possible that your other children are not overweight? Odds are your parental resources are already stretched to the limit, how can you possibly enforce the new rules or start cooking separate meals? Plus, you're not the only one in charge. What about dad, or grandma, or other caregivers who spend significant amounts of time with your child? What about the needs of your other children?

At this point, your head is spinning. The pediatrician spends a few minutes explaining the guidelines to you and may recommend the office nutritionist, and then they move on to see the next patient. You are left completely unprepared to deal with your child, who is melting down, and the struggles that lie ahead.

Obesity is a chronic condition. As of now, there is no cure. It also runs in families. If both parents are overweight, your child has an 80% chance of being obese. Given these statistics, it's highly likely that mom or dad, or both, are also struggling with weight control issues. You are well versed in how hard it is to lose weight and keep it off. Maybe you are still harboring ill feelings from when your own parents tried to control your weight.

Volumes have been written about the detrimental effects of over-controlling parents. Parents find it almost impossible to strike the right balance. My office hours are filled with the perceived injustices adults have suffered as children because of their well-intentioned parents. Parents are blamed if they are too restrictive and if they are not restrictive enough. One pediatrician threatened to call Child Protective Services if the child did not lose weight. Another doctor thought the parents of an obese toddler should be arrested for child abuse. Taking away children or arresting parents cannot be the solution.

This is a complex emotionally charged issue for everyone involved. You, as a parent, need time to process the information and come up with a plan that will work for your child and your family. Ideally, the pediatrician should talk to parents privately. This will allow parents to talk freely with the doctor and avoid undue stress to the child. I know this advice is counter to the opinion currently prevailing in the medical community. Most doctors believe a child should hear the news from a medical professional so the child is more likely to comply. Most parents would also rather the doctor speak to their child so they are not seen as the bad guy.

A mom called me recently for help with her fifteen-year-old daughter. I explained that I don't treat children unless I'm 100% convinced it's the child's idea. The mom was clearly frustrated that, in her view, I wouldn't help. She said, "At least we have a pediatrician appointment soon and he can talk to her." When I told her that all her daughter will hear is, "You think I'm obese," the mom bristled and said, "She's not obese." Maybe not, but that's what she'll hear.

Another distressed mom called me the same week for help with her eleven-year-old son. In this case, the mom was concerned because the doctor told her son Evan that he was obese. This mom immediately asked to speak to the doctor privately to avoid further damage. She expressed her concerns to the doctor and requested that in the future he speak only privately to her about her son's weight. I agreed to work with this mom, without her son present, to help her foster a healthy environment for her son.

My years of experience tell me the medical community is going about this in the wrong way. Nothing good ever comes from telling your child you are worried they are overweight. Pediatricians should talk to families about healthy habits. All families, not just the overweight ones. The recommendations of The American Academy of Pediatrics apply to all children, regardless of weight. It's time we treat all kids the same. Our goal should be optimal health. This includes emotional and mental health. Every effort should be made to avoid the psychological damage and stigma associated with being diagnosed as fat.

CHAPTER 4:

Take a breath

Your children are watching everything you do. If you tell them to eat their vegetables and you don't eat yours, they notice. If you insist they eat breakfast but you never eat breakfast, they notice. If you tense up when they reach for another cookie, they notice. They hear everything you say too, even though it seems they're not listening. Your words are so powerful they can *make* your child fat. A few comments about your child's weight and eating habits are as bad as many comments.

Telling your child not to finish everything on their plate can be just as damaging as forcing them to clean their plate. Carla is the mother of two girls, age seven and eight. Her seven-year-old daughter Alina is very lean. Eight-year-old Jacqueline is morbidly obese. Carla is under a lot of pressure from her pediatrician to get Jacqueline's weight down. One afternoon Carla was taking an online quiz with Jacqueline nearby. The question was, "What does Mommy always say?" Her daughter responded, "You don't have to eat everything on your plate." This seems like good practical advice. It certainly seems better than the mean-spirited mealtime refrain, "Even a train stops sometimes," that another client of mine grew up hearing. Both comments send the same message: you're getting fat, and it's a problem.

Commenting on how much your child is eating has been positively correlated with BMI, which means that these mealtime teachable moments may be contributing to your child's weight gain. So, when you say, "stop shoveling it in," "slow down," or "take a breath" to your child, you are not teaching better table manners. You are letting them know you think they are eating too much which translates into, "You think I'm fat." Once your child thinks you think they are fat, they are much more likely to become fat, regardless of their starting BMI.

We all want our children to be their best versions of themselves. It is our job as parents to safely shepherd our children into adulthood. If your child starts gaining weight and you don't say anything, aren't you being negligent? Childhood obesity is linked to a myriad of health issues. Plus, overweight children have historically been picked on and bullied. As parents, we are hardwired to protect our children. The uncomfortable truth is, instead of protecting our children, we may inadvertently become their first bully. Leanne is so concerned that the other boys will make fun of her son Zach's fatty middle, she doesn't realize that every time she calls her son chunky and pinches his extra fat, she is the worst offender.

Danielle's parents are divorced. When she spends time with her dad Rob, he wants to be the fun parent. Rob bakes cookies, takes her out for Chinese food, orders in a pizza. At the same time, he is constantly on Danielle's case to manage her weight with self-control and portion control. Her dad can't understand why she doesn't have more discipline. This has become a huge point of contention between them. As soon as Rob starts talking about portion control, Danielle shuts down. Danielle has always struggled with her weight. Now in her late teens, Danielle weighs over 200 pounds and is prediabetic. All these mini-sermons about her lack of self-control have made Danielle feel bad about herself, which leads her to eat more.

Amy, a vivacious high school senior, vividly recalls the shame she felt when she was having breakfast with her friends and she went to take a second bagel. Her dad asked her if she really needed to eat that. Put on the spot, in front of everybody, Amy felt humiliated. She didn't have the second bagel. Her dad walked away feeling he helped his daughter. Amy still carries this memory and the humiliation with her.

These memories string together to form a constant film reel of criticism in your child's head; a film that will be played over and over again. Eventually, all you will have to do is *look* in their direction and they know what you're thinking. Don't take my word for it, ask your child to show you the look you give them when you think they have eaten too much or are eating something they shouldn't. Joshua, a teenage boy in my practice, rendered his mom speechless with his spot-on imitation of "her look." The mother had been insisting that she never says anything to Joshua about his eating habits. She doesn't have to. The look is as damaging as any words.

It is frustrating not to be able to control your child's weight. Especially when you are being pressured by your child's pediatrician. This frustration can cause parents to lash out at their child. Pam came home from work early one evening and caught her daughter, Carly, in front of the TV with her hand in a bag of chips. Exhausted and at the end of her rope, Pam lost her cool. She turned off the TV, grabbed the chips and yelled, "So this is what you're doing while I'm at work? It's no wonder you're still so fat!" Not surprisingly, Carly screamed, "I hate you!" and stomped off to her room. Pam apologized later that night, but the sting of her words made a lasting imprint on Carly's psyche. Carly no longer felt safe eating openly in her own house. She began to spend more time alone in her room or staying up late so she could eat without the fear of discovery.

If you're not sure that what you're about to say is hurtful, try this simple test. Ask yourself how you would feel if your mother or father or spouse said it to you. Nobody wants to hear they are eating too much or that there is something inherently wrong with their character because they like carbs. If you try to shame your child into losing weight, you are virtually guaranteeing your child will grow up fat and feeling bad about themselves. I've heard parents say, "I know I'm screwing my kid up but I can't help myself," an alarming number of times.

Anything you say to your child about their weight will only make the situation worse. This includes looks.

NOT HELPFUL

- I'm telling you this for your own good.
- If I don't tell you that you are fat, who will?
- If you keep gaining weight, kids will make fun of you.
- You just need a little discipline, willpower, self-control.
- Did you really need to eat that?
- I think you've eaten enough.
- Don't eat that.
- Are you sure you should eat that?
- Eat broccoli instead of that.
- You're not really hungry.
- Are you eating again?
- Naturally, I think you're beautiful, but....
- If you lose weight you'll have more confidence.
- I just want you to be happy.
- If you're good you can have a cookie.
- You're sad, have a cookie.
- You can't have dessert unless you eat your vegetables.
- I just want you to be healthy.
- Are you going to the gym today?
- You should go to the gym because you ate that cake.
- You're going in the wrong direction.
- You should eat more like your sister.
- It's just baby fat.

- You're not fat, you're chunky.
- Watch it, you don't want to get fat like Aunt Dora.
- You have those genes, you know.
- Sorry, you inherited my fat thighs, knees, ankles.
- You have such a pretty face.
- Good, you have a stomach bug, maybe you'll lose a few pounds.

Chapter 5:

Parents must be on the same page

At this point, it should be getting clearer that not only is it impossible to control your child's weight, but any overt attempts you make will only make the problem worse. The next hurdle is convincing the other important adults in your child's life to get on board. This is a biggie. Even if your child only sees the aunties a few times a year, their comments and looks can have a big impact. Take Carmella, for example. She refused to spend summers in Puerto Rico with her aunts and cousins because every time she arrived they would say, "Oh, look! You're getting so juicy." Then there's Rhonda, who dreaded visiting her great aunts in Miami because they would assess her weight as she came down the airport escalator.

The people closest to us can be the hardest to convince. The truth is, maybe you're not even 100 percent convinced. Even if you agree with me in theory, on some level you may be relieved someone else in your child's life is "dealing with it." Kind of like hedging your bets. This could mean looking the other way like Bryn and Jon do every time their family visits Jon's dad, Grandpa Joe. Grandpa has the habit of poking their eight-year-old daughter Kat's belly while saying, "Look at the pot on her." As Bryn is relaying the story to me, she is disturbed but also resigned to Grandpa Joe's behavior. Bryn has asked Jon to tell his dad to cut it out but to no avail. Bryn tells me Grandpa Joe also does this to Jon so it's harmless, right? Wrong, it's not harmless! It is our job as parents to protect our children. Even if it means protecting them from a grandpa who has no filter.

When I met the Wilson family, both parents were significantly overweight and their son was already flagged by the pediatrician as obese. Between work, school and sports, this super busy family relied on takeout food during the week and went out for every meal over the weekend. Their cabinets were packed with chips, cookies, and candy. Over-ordering and overeating was the norm. They called me in because they were ready for a change. I went to their house, held a family meeting, decluttered the snack cabinets, and helped them devise a plan. We didn't talk about weight. We focused on grocery shopping, meal preparation, and relying less on take-out food.

The mom, Kim, was on board. The dad, Bill, not so much. Kim began to cook more meals at home. She bought more fruits and veggies, and less junk. The children started eating more fruits and veggies. Everyone was on board but Bill and Grandma. Bill unapologetically sabotaged Kim's efforts by bringing in bagels, pies, and ice cream. Grandma, who was always on Kim's case about her weight, continued to stop by with donuts and cupcakes because how could a grandma show up empty handed?

Without Bill on board, Kim's frustration grew. The final straw came when Kim cooked a chicken dish for dinner that nobody wanted to eat. Instead of supporting Kim's efforts, Bill went out to get pizza for the family. Feeling defeated, Kim gave up and went back to her old habits.

A few months go by when I get a call from Bill. He's had a health scare and is ready to make a change. I start working with Bill and he is now down forty pounds. Now Kim is the saboteur, bringing home unhealthy and hard to resist foods. It seems impossible for them to be on the same page at the same time. The mixed messages they are sending have been picked up by their children. The kids know how to work the system, and their supply of junk food has remained constant.

Drill sergeant dads can be just as much a problem as junk food dads. I received a call from a take-charge dad recently. It's a little unusual for a dad to call me, but he explains that the mom works long hours and so he is going to handle this. He introduces himself and lets me know I have already helped his older daughter reach her fitness goals. He wants to know if I can help his younger daughter Cassidy. Cassidy is thirteen, lives on junk food, and she is getting chubby. On the surface, this seems like a reasonable request. All I need to do is give his daughter a basic nutrition lesson, something along the lines of instead of eating junk food, try to eat more fruits, vegetables and lean protein. Problem solved. But it's never that simple.

The dad is stumped when I asked him if his daughter wants to see me. His daughter's readiness to change hasn't even occurred to him. He was looking to me for a lifeline and he is genuinely surprised when I turn him away. I was only able to help his older daughter because she found me, drove herself to my office, and was motivated to make a change. A short time later he calls back to let me know Cassidy said she would see me, and I reluctantly agree. When they arrive in my office, Cassidy has her arms folded over her chest in a defensive posture. I ask her, as I always do in these situations if she is being held hostage here against her will. It seems obvious to me that she does not, in fact, want to be here. It also becomes clear that drill sergeant dad cannot relate to his daughter's emotional relationship with food or her seeming lack of willpower. He views her overeating as a sign of weakness and poor character. I am unable to establish a connection with Cassidy or her father, and the meeting does not go well.

A few months later the mom calls me to ask for help and, again, I reluctantly agree. When they arrive it's apparent that

Cassidy still does not want to be here. Through the ensuing conversation, I discover that nothing has changed since our first meeting. Neither parent is willing to cook dinner. The house is still stocked with soda, energy drinks, frozen pizza, and every junky snack you can imagine. Cassidy's parents can't agree on who is responsible for providing healthier food at home, but they do agree that Cassidy is fat and it's a problem.

Before starting a family, most couples spend hours discussing how they want to raise their kids. These discussions typically include thoughts on religion, childcare, schooling, and discipline styles, but what about health and fitness philosophies? Even if you did discuss your fitness philosophies in advance, circumstances change. Marriages can end. Parents can remarry. Children may split time between two houses. There may be stepparents and siblings in the picture. Caregivers and babysitters can have an influential role as well. Grandma might be responsible for cooking the family meals. It seems almost impossible to get everyone involved on the same page. I know one little boy who would go to his next-door neighbor's house after school and help himself to everything in their pantry as if it were his own home.

The goal here should be to recruit, not to crucify. We have all made mistakes, so pointing out every transgression is not helpful. Here are my suggestions for talking with family members and caregivers about how they can help foster a healthier home environment for your children with a unified approach.

- Start on a positive note by pointing out anything they may already be doing that is helpful.

- Expect resistance. As with any new and radical idea, it is going to take more than one conversation to persuade them to make a change.

- Be clear about what you are asking and why it's important. This is not a favor for you, but something to help the whole family.

- Prioritize. Pick one thing to work on first. It could be to stop micromanaging mealtime, stop making any comments about what your child is eating, or to stop going to fast food restaurants.

- Be kind. This is an emotionally charged issue that often goes back to childhood. Be sensitive to where they may be coming from.

- Be appreciative. Praise lavishly when you observe them doing what you have asked them to do.

CHAPTER 6:

How much junk is in the house?

Grandma shows up with moon pies. A visiting neighbor brings a box of donuts. The dad buys two bags of chips because they were buy one, get one free. Your child comes home with a stash of candy from a birthday party. The supply of junk food in your house is endless, or maybe you don't let any junk food enter your house. Either way, your child ends up chubby. There is no simple solution or one right answer about what to do with all this junk. The environment you grow up in does influence your behavior. Your household junk food policy, if you even have one, is typically based on your own exposure to junk food as a child and how you believe that affected your weight and relationship with food.

Mia grew up in a house where her mom was a "health nut" and there was a strict no junk food policy. This made Mia feel deprived and she became that kid who devoured junky snacks every time she went to a friend's house. We all know a child similar to Mia, but Mia's story has a twist. Mia's dad did not share her mom's zealous health food views, and when her parents got divorced her dad stocked his house with all the yummy forbidden foods Mia craved. Monday through Friday Mia ate healthy with her mom and on weekends she spent with her dad, the floodgates opened. As a grown woman with children of her own, Mia is repeating this pattern from her childhood. Monday through Friday she eats "clean" and the weekends are one long cheat meal. Mia's dysfunctional relationship with food is affecting her family as she finds herself struggling to find the right balance with her own children.

Mia's daughter, Jessie, is not that interested in food. Jessie's weight is hovering in the bottom 25th percentile compared to other children her age. Her brother, Jake, has an insatiable appetite. As Jake's weight topples the growth charts, his pediatrician is on Mia's case to do something. At age eight, Jake already has his own nutritionist. Mia knows firsthand the damage that can be done by growing up in an overly restrictive household, but she is under a lot of pressure to get her son's weight under control. The pediatrician chastises Mia for bringing junk food into the house. Visits to the pediatrician are very stressful.

Many in the dietitian community, especially those who work with disordered eating, believe food should never be restricted and even find the term junk food derisive. The theory is, the more a food is made taboo, the more children will want to eat it. As a society, we are distrustful of people who try to raise their children without junk food. It seems un-American. My cousin Laura kept only organic, unprocessed whole foods in her house decades before organic became a household term. Laura belonged to a food co-op, baked her own bread, and made every effort to feed her two boys in the most healthful way. Family lore has it, that one day her husband was left in charge of feeding the children. He stopped at a gas station to pick up white bread and hot dogs for their lunch. My Aunt, the boy's grandmother, tells this story gleefully. Grandma doesn't want her grandsons to grow up without knowing the pleasure of eating junk food. Junk food is such a part of our national identity that you seem "weird" if you don't eat it and deprived if you're not allowed to eat it.

The dictionary definition of junk food is food that has low nutritional value, typically produced in the form of packaged snacks needing little or no preparation. There is also a subset of junk food marketed towards the more health-conscious consumer. In other words, these snacks *sound* healthy but really aren't. This includes snacks like baked chips, Veggie Straws, "smart" popcorn, pita chips, rice cakes, and 100-calorie packs. None of these snacks are nutrient dense, or what most nutritionists would consider healthy.

Think of junk food in terms of being sessionable, a term food companies have borrowed from beer makers. Beer is considered sessionable if it's suitable for a lengthy drinking session. Likewise, junk food has been formulated to keep you eating until the bag is empty. Not everyone who starts eating a bag of chips, can't stop, but that's not for the food companies' lack of trying. Junk food, like cigarettes, can be highly addictive. Just the right combination of fat, sugar, and salt make it difficult to stop eating most junk foods, once you've had that first taste.

Food addiction is a real and serious problem. The question is, does how much junk food you keep in your house determine the odds of your child growing up to be a food addict? Maybe it's not the amount of junk in your house, but it's your attitude towards it. Or is it possible that we don't have as much control over it as we think? Karen grew up in a house always fully stocked with all kinds of food. The kind of house where kids came to raid the cabinets and eat all the foods not allowed in their own houses. Karen has always credited her take-it-or-leave-it attitude towards junk food to having grown up surrounded by it. She never had to secretly binge on junk food for fear it would be taken away, or that she would be scolded for eating it. Karen's sister Valerie, on the other hand, has always struggled with her weight. For years Valerie blamed her weight problem on being surrounded by junk food as a child, yet she keeps junky snacks in the house for her own family. Once again, one approach does not fit all.

Now Karen has a family of her own. Happy with her relationship with food, she set out to recreate it for her family. Karen's house is always fully stocked with all kinds of food. The theory is, if junky snacks are always around, you build up a tolerance to their seductive nature. This seemed to work for Karen's son who has a relaxed relationship with junk food, but her daughter, Miranda, is constantly snack seeking. As Miranda's weight escalates, Karen is now questioning her junk food policy. Karen knows that once you gain weight it's nearly impossible to lose it, so it seems logical to educate Miranda on the value of different foods and on being more mindful when eating. Maybe Miranda doesn't realize that there is limited nutritional value in a New York bagel, or that the local Chinese restaurant gives you way too much food for the lunch special. Despite her best intentions, any suggestions Karen makes to her daughter about healthy snacks, portion size, or nutrition information are met with resistance.

Karen followed the rules. Junky snacks were not made taboo. Yet, while cleaning Miranda's room, Karen finds scores of candy wrappers and discarded chip bags under Miranda's bed. Does Miranda have a hoarding disorder or a binge eating disorder? Maybe she is just your average teenage slob. As a parent, it is hard to watch your child engage in self-destructive behavior. There must be something parents can do. Even if it were possible for Karen to positively impact Miranda's relationship with food, that window has closed now that Miranda has a car and spending money of her own. Miranda's friends are now her biggest influence. Like many teenage girls, they spend their free time watching videos and eating snacks.

Bruce grew up in a house with two obese parents and junk food readily available. Overeating at every meal was the norm. Bruce learned to eat a lot and to eat fast because if he wasn't quick enough his father would eat his food. Bruce developed a binge eating disorder fueled by his anxiety that is triggered by food insecurity. He is constantly eating to deal with stress and to dull uncomfortable emotions. As an adult, Bruce's weight has reached 400 pounds. Bruce wonders how much of his struggle with obesity is attributed to his genetics, his home environment, and his parents' attitude toward food. Was Bruce doomed to be obese, or could it have been prevented? What about Bruce's children? Our relationship with food is complicated and often tangled up with feelings of love and security. Even the most well-intentioned parents find it nearly impossible to break the cycle.

Diane has one child, Samantha. Diane was determined to feed her daughter only the healthiest, most wholesome foods. Diane proudly recalls that she never even gave Samantha jarred baby food. All her food was organic and pureed at home. When Samantha was old enough for preschool, Diane sent her with cut up kiwis and grapes for a snack. That is until the school called and implored her to pack goldfish or pretzels for Samantha. It seems Samantha was stealing her classmate's more appealing snacks. Are we inadvertently turning our kids into thieves? One girl I know, an honor student, stole her mom's car when she was thirteen so she could buy forbidden ice cream.

What are parents supposed to do? There is no denying that parents are blamed if their child is overweight. They are blamed by relatives, medical professionals, and even strangers. Restricting your child's food intake is widely seen as abusive, but so is feeding your child too much junk. One local pediatrician threatened to call Child Protective Services on a mother who continued to give her obese child junk food. Grandparents feel they have the right to intervene for the child's own good. Total strangers pass judgment if a chubby kid is allowed ice cream. Everyone seems to have an opinion.

Choice architecture studies how the environment nudges behavior. One of the findings of these studies is that it is human nature to pick the default option or the option that is already decided for you. At home, make fruit the default option by keeping a bowl stocked with washed fruit on the counter. If you also have cookies and chips in the house, keep them in the cabinet so your children need to work a little harder to get to them. By making healthier food the default option, you are increasing the odds that your children will eat it.

5 Tips

1. Snacks are not meal replacements. Be skeptical of Pop Tarts, granola bars, protein bars, and other snacks marketed as meals.

2. Don't overlook liquids like juice and soda. These are high in sugar with few, if any, nutrients.

3. Keep snacks in cabinets and off the counter.

4. It's appropriate to make the rule that eating is only in the kitchen or dining room, and not in the bedroom or in front of the TV.

5. If you really don't want your children to eat something, don't buy it. Once you bring something into the house, it is fair game for them to eat it.

CHAPTER 7:

Does this dress make me look fat?

Fifteen-year-old Sara spends hours in front of the mirror inspecting her body from every angle. She wonders if her butt is too big and if her stomach is a little poochy. Sara badgers her mom at least ten times a day with the same question: "Am I fat?" In the next breath, Sara might beg to order in a pizza. It takes every ounce of self-control Sara's mom, Becky, has not to shout, "If you're so worried about being fat, why on Earth do you want to order a pizza?" The thing is, Sara is not really asking if she's fat. She is not looking to be fixed. Sara just wants reassurance that she is OK. In this case, offering diet advice to your child is not helpful. It only validates what they suspect, that there is something wrong with them.

You know this is true if you ever asked the question, "Does this dress make me look fat?" If your partner says yes, you're steaming mad because of their insensitivity. If they say, no, you accuse them of lying. You are not really looking for an honest response, just reassurance that you are OK. If you've asked this in front of your child or, worse, to your child, you're increasing the odds that they grow up dissatisfied with their own bodies. A mom is the most beautiful person in the world to her child. If you're critical of how you look, how is your child supposed to be happy with how they look? It is not enough to tell your child how beautiful or graceful or special they are. How a child feels about themselves is correlated to how you feel about yourself. Four-year-old Ruby watches her mom weigh herself every morning. After her mom gets off the scale, either happy or unhappy, Ruby hops on the scale and asks her mom, "Am I beautiful?" Modeling behavior that is consistent with a positive body image is crucial to raise confident children with healthy self-esteem. Besides forcing your loved one to look at you in a critical way, there is no satisfying answer to "does this make me look fat?" Stop asking the question.

Not only girls struggle with this. Tyler is generally a confident kid. Trying on clothes for middle school, however, turned into a fiasco when his favorite team jersey was too tight around his middle. When your child is miserable, it is natural to offer advice. In this case, telling Tyler to do sit-ups or to lay off the snacks is not the advice he needs. The focus should not be that Tyler's belly is too big, but that the shirt is too small. Simply offer to replace it. If he insists on wearing the tight shirt anyway, let him. The less you engage with this conversation the better.

Sam, an active eight-year-old boy, is being teased at camp for having man boobs, common slang for gynecomastia. The other boys are laughing, pointing, even pinching. If Sam were a girl, the mom, Deb's, course of action would be swift and clearly defined. The camp director would be called immediately and stern disciplinary action would be taken. The fact that Sam is a boy should not cloud his mom's judgment--harassment is harassment--but it does. Instead of focusing on the kids who bullied her son, Deb focuses on making Sam less of a target. She tells him, "If you don't like the teasing, do something about the man boobs."

As parents, our instincts are always to protect our children. It's understandable why Deb wants to help her son fix this problem. "Man boobs" are generally seen as undesirable and shameful. Many boys swim with their shirts on or avoid the pool altogether because they don't want to subject themselves to ridicule. However, by suggesting in this vulnerable moment that Sam should be doing certain exercises or eating less junk food, it seems like Deb is siding with the bullies. By doing so she is inadvertently validating the idea that there is something wrong with her son. A better approach might be to let Sam know that he is fine, it's the bullies who need fixing. Gynecomastia is not only caused by obesity, but can be brought on by puberty or a hormone imbalance. Exercise or a diet change may not always improve this condition. If you are concerned about it, ask your pediatrician for treatment options.

Nobody wants their child to be teased. Going through adolescence is hard enough without body image issues. Body image is the subjective lens that you use to view your physical self. It has very little to do with how much you weigh or what size clothes you wear. Parents can inadvertently cause lasting damage to their child's body image. One mom brought her beautiful daughter Ellie to my practice the summer between middle and high school. The mom looked at her daughter, made some very dramatic hand gestures and said, "She can't go to high school looking misshapen like this." I sat there in stunned silence. Sadly, this is not even an unusual occurrence.

I routinely get calls from mothers interested in having their children lose weight. The mothers think that losing weight will help their children gain more confidence. The reality is trying to get your child to lose even five pounds can shake their confidence. It doesn't take much to plant the seeds for poor body image. Confidence, like body image, has very little to with a number on the scale. How you feel about yourself is a much better confidence indicator than how you look. The kids in high school that project supreme confidence become the popular kids. Objectively, these kids are not different than the rest of the student body. They may not even be what we traditionally think of as great looking. What makes them stand out is that they believe they are worthy of the school's attention and love. They are projecting confidence, so that's what we see. On Facebook, I once posted, "Skinny girls look good in clothes, fit girls look good naked." A wise Facebook user rightly called me out on the post. His comment was, "Regardless of topography, happy girls look good in clothes *and* naked." He's right. Happiness with yourself is beautiful, but, unfortunately, way too rare.

Poking fun at yourself or pointing out your flaws is a common defense mechanism. You've probably noticed that an overweight comedian will always start the set with a fat joke to beat the audience to the punch. As parents, how we speak about ourselves affects how our children speak about themselves. Consequently, if you walk around saying how fat you are, you should not be surprised when your mini-me does the same. When I met Brenda, a curvy mother of two boys, she told me she always tells her overweight son how fat she is so he will feel better about himself. Denigrating yourself is never a winning strategy. Brenda came to me to see how she could help her son. The first thing I told her to do was stop disparaging herself. Not just in front of her son, but to stop period.

Recently I was taking a health coaching course and the instructor asked, "If you were a car what car would you be?" I said I would be a shiny new BMW. Just by saying that, I felt like a shiny new BMW. Words are powerful. If you say something enough, that's what you become. Even if you're feeling like a broken-down jalopy, dream big. If you can't even imagine it, how can it possibly happen?

Body language speaks volumes about how you feel about yourself. Do you walk around with your arms crossed over your chest like you have something to hide? Do you slouch in a defensive posture? Do you miss out on family fun because you don't want to wear a bathing suit? Are you putting your life on hold until you reach your elusive goal weight? Children are programmed to pick up on all these cues. We can't expect them to do something we can't even do.

Confidence Boosting Tips

There is no downside to feeling good about yourself. Having a positive body image does not mean you are conceited. I am in awe daily of what my body can do.

Try these tips to increase your confidence and create a positive body image:

- Focus on the positive. Spend time each day appreciating your body for its amazing qualities.

- Stop insulting yourself. Not another word. Not aloud or to yourself. I'm a shiny new BMW because I want to be.

- Exercise not because you are trying to change your body or punish it. Move your body to feel alive.

- Stop comparing yourself to others. There will always be someone in better shape than you. Who cares? Why should you feel bad about yourself if your neighbor wears a size smaller than you? What a waste of energy!

CHAPTER 8:

Resist the urge to...

It's not too late to change course. Every single one of us has done some if not all these things. You already know these strategies are ineffective. As parents, we are programmed to help. We want to fix things. Children are programmed to please us, though sometimes they rebel. Helping and fixing and pleasing and rebelling are no match for unwanted weight gain. The best way to help your child is to stop all this helping.

RESIST THE URGE TO:

- **Give diet advice - solicited or unsolicited**

Recently I overheard two of my boys having a heated debate on what it means to eat healthy. Nobody asked my opinion and I didn't give it. Even if it seems like your child is asking you for diet advice, don't do it.

- **Offer to go on a diet with your child**

If you are a lifelong dieter, you already know diets are ineffective. Looking back, most dieters wish they weigh now what they weighed before they went on their first diet. Your child has witnessed you diet and fail. Going on a diet for a few weeks or months and then reverting to your normal eating habits only reinforces how futile dieting is.

- ## Put your child on a diet

It is unfair and unreasonable to expect a child, whose executive functioning is not fully developed, to do something most adults cannot do.

- ## Announce or overtly go on a diet yourself

We pass our habits and our relationship with food on to our children. Chronic dieting is not the behavior we want our kids to emulate. Ellen is either always on a diet, which means prepackaged meals and no carbs, or off a diet. When Ellen is off her diet, she gorges herself on everything her dieting-self was denied. Ellen has three teenage daughters; two of them are exhibiting signs of repeating this same dysfunctional pattern. The third is determined to go in a different, more healthy direction. All three are reacting to what they see at home.

- ## Weigh your child, or weigh yourself in front of your child

If you must weigh yourself, do it in private. Getting weighed is not a family activity. Do not force or encourage your child to step on the scale. This only reinforces the idea that their worth is weight dependent.

- ## Bring your child to a nutritionist for weight control

Nutritionists have no secret weapons or magic tricks. Teaching your child about healthy eating is not my job, it's yours; and not through your words, but your *actions*. Alice came to see me about her own weight and she also had some concerns about her seven-year-old daughter. I have a plate on my desk that shows the portion sizes of protein, vegetables, and a side dish. Alice said she wants to bring her daughter to see me so she can see the portion plate. If you want your child to get a better idea of serving size, serve them dinner restaurant style with the food already plated, instead of family style with the food in serving dishes in the center. If you bring your child to a nutritionist, it will only reinforce that you think there is something wrong with them.

- **Treat your children differently**

I know every child is different, but urging one to eat more and the other to eat less is a recipe for disaster. Jan is the mother of two boys, Justin and Frankie. Justin has special needs and many food aversions. His brother, Frankie, has a robust appetite and his weight is creeping into the 95th percentile which is the clinical definition of obesity. Jan came to see me for guidance. Frankie already feels that Justin is getting preferential treatment. It is doubly unfair that Justin is allowed dessert and is encouraged to eat all the foods Frankie is told to limit. It seems reasonable to treat these brothers differently because they have different needs, but this strategy never has the intended effect and only results in feelings of resentment. A better approach is to take a step back and let your children determine for themselves when they have had enough to eat.

- **Weigh your child with your eyes**

It doesn't matter if your child is sixteen or sixty, they can tell you are judging them by how much they weigh. Maddy's mom's eyes are so accurate she can detect even a one-pound fluctuation in Maddy's weight. Your child can sense your approval or disapproval even if you don't comment out loud.

- **Send mixed messages**

Try to be as consistent as possible. Noah's mom lets him know he is dangerously overweight one minute, but in the next minute, she is pushing food on him. Melissa's mom, Donna, is a habitual dieter. Donna sends a constant stream of mixed messages to Melissa as she urges Melissa to eat all the food she is denying herself. Donna's rationale is that because Melissa is lean, she should enjoy all the food Donna isn't allowed to eat. Mixed messages are confusing and can cause damage regardless of your child's weight.

- **Be restrictive with food**

If you bring food into the house it's fair game. You can't be upset with your child for eating the food you provide. Likewise, if you take your child to a burger place, don't be surprised when they order a burger and fries.

- **Condemn foods for being fattening**

I grew up hearing my mom say, "This is so fattening I really shouldn't eat it." Eat it or don't eat it, Mom, but stop talking about it.

- **Criticize your own body**

You're the most beautiful person in the world to your children. If you're not happy with how you look, how can they possibly be happy with how they look? From this moment on, vow not to say another disparaging word about your physical appearance. Not one.

- **Pay or otherwise bribe your child to lose weight**

I know parents who have offered to pay their children up to $100 per pound lost or to buy them a car or take them on a trip if they reach their goal weight. This strategy doesn't promote weight loss, just more negative emotions and hurt feelings.

- **Give your child a message gift**

When Izzy was going to college her mom offered to give her an exercise bike. Izzy's incredulous response was, "OMG, You think I'm fat!" When Anna's dad showed up at Christmas with a fistful of cash to buy her a gym membership, she said, "I know you think I'm fat, Dad." Unless your child specifically asks for an exercise-related gift, do not give one.

- **Talk about how good or bad someone looks if they gain or lose weight**

When your child overhears you say how bad your Aunt Harriet looks because she gained weight, you are teaching your child it's OK to judge others and themselves based on weight.

- **Comment on your child's body**

Rebecca's mom told her, "You're built like me so you're going to have to watch the carbs and sweets. Already your butt is getting too big." Rebecca went on a strict diet to shrink her butt. Even as she was getting dangerously thin, everyone kept telling her how great she looked. Rebecca starved herself to the point of hospitalization. Now she is at a healthy weight but is struggling with body image issues. She can't get past the idea that she is disappointing her parents for not being thin. If you praise your child for looking great when they lose weight, what happens when they gain the weight back?

Chapter 9:

Relationships can be repaired

We all have parenting moments we regret, that doesn't make us bad parents, just human ones. The good news is relationships can be repaired. My goals are the same as yours. I want your kids to be fit and healthy, emotionally and physically.

WHAT YOU CAN DO:

- **Assess the situation**

Take an honest look at how you approach diet and weight loss and what effect this may have had on your child. Are you already finding hidden wrappers under their bed? Has there already been a failed attempt at Weight Watchers or another diet? Have meal times become a battle about what and how much your child should eat? Has your child already been to see a nutritionist under protest and duress?

- **Open dialogue**

Ask your child what they think about how you have approached their weight and diet in the past. Don't argue each point. Really listen to what your child is trying to tell you. Look at what their body language is telling you. This is not a conversation about healthy eating and weight. Nor should it be about how unhealthy it is to be fat or how you just want to help.

- **Be authentic**

It's OK to admit you were wrong. Be honest. Your intentions are good. You never meant to be hurtful. You can say that.

- **Show empathy**

Your child may already be feeling pressure to conform to a certain physical ideal from friends, TV, or social media. Home should be a safe place. Let your child know you love and accept them.

- **Re-establish trust**

Relationship building takes time. Be consistent so your child feels secure that you are approaching things differently.

- **Recognize and praise**

Children are constantly looking for your approval. You can recognize and validate their accomplishments without tying them to weight, physical appearance, or willpower.

- **Have patience**

Don't lose sight of your endgame. Your child's emotional and mental health is just as important as their physical health. Making a lasting change is hard for you and your child.

- **Practice acceptance**

Some things, OK, most things, are out of our control. You can't control everything your child eats. Ultimately your child becomes responsible for their choices.

- **Explore your own issues**

Our attitudes and beliefs about parenting often stem from our own childhood. We either want to recreate our childhoods or are determined to do things differently. Unresolved issues from your own childhood may cloud your judgment when it comes to raising your children. It's worth taking the time to explore how these unresolved issues may be influencing you.

- **Establish new rituals and routines**

Dana wakes up in the middle of the night and has pig out parties with her three-year-old daughter Lily. Dana tells me, "This is our special time. Lily loves this time." Dana knows she is perpetuating unhealthy habits, but a part of her doesn't want to lose this special time with her daughter. With a little creativity, new family rituals can be established that don't revolve around food.

- **Be a good role model**

It's never too late to start modeling the behavior you want to foster in your child. This doesn't mean being preachy or making a big show of your new healthy eating or exercise routine. Keep your mouth shut and do the right thing. Your children will notice.

- **Forgive**

We have all been hurt, made mistakes, and said things we regret. Anger, blame, and resentments keep us from moving forward. Forgive those who hurt you and apologize to those you may have hurt.

CHAPTER 10:

Moving forward

Up until now, the methods we have tried to control our children's weight have relied mainly on extrinsic motivation. Extrinsic motivation is when we do something not because we want to, but to please someone else or to get a reward. Parents either reward or punish children to change their behavior, much like we do for our pets. This carrot and stick approach may work wonders for your dog but has limited value when trying to create lasting behavioral changes in your children. In fact, it often has the exact opposite of the intended effect. Basically, your home life becomes more stressful and your child keeps gaining weight.

Intrinsic motivation is when we want to do something for its own sake, not because someone else is pressuring us. When you tap into your intrinsic motivation, your odds of achieving what you set out to do improve dramatically. It makes sense that for your child to have long term success in changing eating habits, *they* must own it, not you. The more you try to bribe or punish your child into complying, the less likely they are to own their behavior. Your best option is to continue to provide a loving, safe environment for your child to grow and flourish. Self-determination and autonomy are basic needs and are necessary for sustained change. You can make your child practice an instrument, but forcing them to practice won't foster a love of music or make them a great musician. An internal drive must be sparked. The same is true for fitness.

Fitness is catching. I've talked a lot about setting a good example. What does that mean exactly? Take your turn, find joy in movement. Don't moan about going to the gym or for a hike. Just do it. If you are going to eat a piece of cake, eat it without commentary about your lack of willpower. Children are watching everything you do; that's how they learn. Don't be surprised that your kids need to eat dinner every night. Every night! Guess what? You need dinner too. Be prepared; have a plan. If it's 4:30 pm and you don't know what's for dinner, it's too late. It doesn't have to be fancy or complicated, it just needs to be done.

If you want your child to try new foods, expand your palate and try some new foods yourself. I have been seeing a mother and her recent college grad daughter for over a year. They have a beautiful relationship with an open line of communication. When I first met them, the daughter, Tamara, was unwilling to try new foods and had a very typical American teenage diet consisting mainly of white carbs and burgers. It recently came to light that her mom is practically phobic about trying new foods. It's no wonder Tamara's diet is so limited! But, now Tamara has a boyfriend that she describes as a foodie. After some initial trepidation, Tamara has started to move out of her comfort zone and is becoming quite the adventurous eater.

Look, family is our first influence but friends are the family we choose. Over time, your children's friends have more and more influence. This is important because research shows you really are only as fit as who you hang around with. I always ask my clients who the fittest person in their life is. Some people can't even come up with one name. Not one! I'm not telling you to go find your child some fit friends. I'm saying you never know who or what will spark their imagination and open their eyes to what is possible, and what they can accomplish. Our friends help us grow and change and determine who we are.

Here is my story. I thank my seventeen-year-old self every day for believing I could be a runner. I was not an athletic child. I was much more likely to be picked last for gym teams than first. When I was a senior in high school I took a gym class in jogging. All the other girls in the class, except for me and a girl named Jane, cut across the grass instead of running around the track. I liked Jane and our friend groups overlapped, but we were not close friends until that class. We chatted and ran, and ran and chatted. With each mile, our friendship grew, and I started to gain confidence and feel like an athlete. That jogging class, that I took as a second semester senior in high school, awoke something in me I didn't know I had.

When I was in my twenties and living in NYC, my college friend Roni said she was going to train for the NYC marathon. Her sister, Erika, had run it the year before. Erika, just a regular person running the marathon, made it seem possible to Roni that she could run one too. When Roni told me, she was training for the marathon, I took one look at her and said, "If you can do it, I can do it." I went from thinking I was unathletic because I was picked last in gym class, to running marathons. I took control of my narrative and started being who I wanted to be, not a reflection of what others thought I could be. Ultimately, you get to determine how you want to live your life. I chose a life of fitness, and it wasn't an obvious choice. Running the marathon changed me, made me feel I could do anything. Ask yourself, what is the hardest thing you've ever done? How did it change you, make you more resilient, stronger? Tap into that strength now as you are trying to change your approach to managing your child's weight.

The dieting paradigm of our mothers' generation doesn't work for me. Dieting doesn't really work for anyone. Trying to somehow get our children to eat less so they won't get fat is sending a counterproductive message. I want my children to think they can do anything, not think there is something wrong with them for eating cake. Few things seem worse to me than purposefully going through life feeling deprived and hungry. Diets fail because they are unsustainable by design. We go on diets and then off them. Anyone who has ever been on a diet knows that once you go off it, you gain the weight you lost back, usually with interest. Dieting has a 95% failure rate. Why would you subject your child to something that is destined to fail? How can we possibly ask our children to do something we can't even do?

A lifestyle change differs from a diet because it is sustainable. The lifestyle you choose isn't one thing, it's *everything*. What does living a fit life mean to you? If you were to live life like a fit person, what changes would you need to make? This is not about deprivation, this is about living your best life, the one you choose. Success brings more success.

Do you remember the girl from the introduction? The one who was fat-shamed by her mom? She is a fit person today not because her mom was always on her case about her weight but despite that. Please do not take this as an endorsement of fat-shaming or use this as evidence that, because she turned out "OK," her mother's methods "worked" and should be emulated. Far from it. True, she broke free by moving away and finding her own path, but she still struggles with issues related to self-worth and weight. It's time to break the generational dieting cycle by recognizing what we thought was the solution, is the problem. We are passing obesity on to our children not necessarily from our genes but from our mindsets.

The idea that you can control your child's weight, that you should do everything possible to get their weight under control, is the problem, not the solution. I know it is terrifying to cede control, but it is also liberating once you accept that you were never in control. In effect, you are not actually giving up control but merely the *idea* of control. This is not a message of despair, but one of hope. Let go of what is not working, what has never worked. The only way for your children to move forward is for you to take a step back. Do it for yourself. Do it for your children. Do it for your children's children.

Acknowledgments

Writing this book would not have been possible without the love and support of my parents, Pepie and Howard Goldman, who raised me to believe I can do anything. Mom, I know you may not agree entirely with my point of view, but it means so much to me that you are still proud of me for realizing my dream of becoming an author.

I want to thank my editor and friend Susan Mootz Vachris for being a nutrition major at Cornell just long enough for us to meet, before switching to her true calling, English. I'm eternally grateful to you (in no particular order) for your impeccable grammar, style, insight, friendship, and for introducing me to Esther.

When I told my friend Jane Brickner that I was finally going to write this book she offered to be an early reader. I hesitated before accepting her generous offer because I was worried my writing wouldn't live up to her high standards. Jane, thank you for believing in me and for the hours of conversation and counsel that became the basis for this book. I treasure your friendship.

Thank you, Allison Tannenbaum for reentering my life at the exact right time. It's incredible what we have accomplished, rebuilding our dietetics careers from ashes, becoming speakers at FNCE and NYSAND, and building robust private practices. I would not be where I am today without your friendship and support.

Roni McGuire, we have a long history of helping each other reach the finish line. The endless hours we have spent hashing and rehashing has helped me crystalize the ideas in this book. Shine on and glow, my beautiful friend, the best is yet to come.

Thank you, Nancy Greene, for generously allowing me to include your Oprah poem in my book. I admire you and your commitment to always living your best life. Even though I'm the big sister, it often seems our roles are reversed. I love you Sissy. You are my person.

Finally, I would like to thank my children Jacob, Ari, Ben, and Danny for their free spirits and beautiful hearts. I don't know how I got so lucky to be your mom.

Notes

Introduction

1. Pulgaron, E. (2013). Childhood Obesity: A Review of Increased Risk for Physical and Psychological Comorbidities. *Clinical Therapeutics, 35*(1), A18-A32.
2. Griffiths LI, Parsons TJ, Hill AJ. Self-esteem and quality of life in obese children and adolescents: a systematic review. *Int J Pediatr Obes.* 2010;5(4):282–304.

Chapter 1

1. Ng, M., Flemming, T., & Robinson, M. (2014). Global, regional, and national prevalence of overweight and obesity in children and adults during 1980-2013: A systemic analysis for the global burden of disease study 2013. *The Lancet, 384*(9945), 766-781.
2. Gill, S., & Panda, S. (2015). A Smartphone App Reveals Erratic Diurnal Eating Patterns in Humans that can be Modulated for Health Benefits. *Cell Metabolism, 22*(5), 789-798.
3. Bilger, M., Kruger, E., & Finkelstein, E. (2017). Measuring Socioeconomic Inequality in Obesity: Looking Beyond the Obesity Threshold. *Health Economics, 26*(8), 1052-1066.
4. Piernas, C., & Popkin, B. M. (2011). Food Portion Patterns and Trends among U.S. Children and the Relationship to Total Eating Occasion Size, 1977-2006. *The Journal of Nutrition, 141*(6), 1159-1164.
5. Children spend only half as much time playing outside as their parents did: National Trust survey. (2016).

6. Hales CM, Carroll MD, Fryar CD, Ogden CL. Prevalence of obesity among adults and youth: United States, 2015–2016. *NCHS Data Brief*. 2017;288:1–8.

Chapter 2

1. McCabe, M., & Ricciardelli, L. (2001). Parent. peer and media influences on body image and strategies to both increase and decrease body size among adolescent boys and girls. *Adolescence,36*(142), 225-240.
2. Fuemmeler, B., Lovelady, C., Zucker, N., & Ostbye, T. (2013). Parental obesity moderates the relationship between childhood appetitive traits and weight. *Obesity, 4*, 815-823.
3. Satter, E. (2008). Secrets of Feeding a Healthy Family: How to eat, How to Raise Good Eaters, How to Cook (2nd ed.). Madison, WI: Kelcy Press.

Chapter 3

1. Daniels, S., & Hassink, S. (2015). The Role of the Pediatrician in Primary Prevention of Obesity. *Pediatrics, 136*(1).
2. Lifshitz, F. (2008). Obesity in Children. *J Clin Res Pediatr Endocrinol,1*(2), 53-60.

Chapter 4

1. Conason, A. (2016, August 16). The Danger of Talking to Children About Weight. Retrieved from psychologytoday.com
2. Cooley, E., Toray, T., Wang, M. C., & Valdez, N. N. (2008). Maternal effects on daughters' eating pathology and body image. *Eating Behaviors, 9*(1), 52-61.
3. Byely, L., Bastiani Archibald, A., Graber, J., & Brooks-Gunn, J. (2000). A prospective study of familial and social influences on girls' body image and dieting.

International Journal of Eating Disorders, 28(2), 155-164.

Chapter 5

1. Hanson, R. (2015, August 10). Parent From the Same Page. Retrieved from psychologytoday.com
2. Hwang, C. (2007, March 7). How to Turn No into Yes! Retrieved from goodhousekeeping.com

Chapter 6

1. Halberstadt, A. (2016, August 21). Letter of Recommendation: Cheddar and Sour Cream Ruffles. *The New York Times Magazine,* 20.
2. Schulte, E., Smeal, J., Lewis, J., & Gearhardt, A. (2018). Development of the Highly Processed Food Withdrawal Scale. *Appetite, 131,* 148-154.
3. Thaler, R. H., & Sunstein, C. R. (2008). *Nudge: Improving decisions about health, wealth, and happiness.* New Haven, CT: Yale University Press.
4. Bucher, T., Collins, C., Rollo, M. E., & McCaffrey, T. A. (2016). Nudging consumers towards healthier choices: A systematic review of positional influences on food choice. *British Journal of Nutrition, 115*(12), 2252-2263.

Chapter 7

1. Hunsinger, D. (2013, August 23). Experts: Mom has biggest impact on girls' body image. *USA Today.* Retrieved from usatoday.com
2. McFadden, J. (2011, August 23). How Mothers Unintentionally Harm Their Daughters' Self-Confidence. Retrieved from huffingtonpost.com
3. Arroyo, A., & Anderson, K. K. (2016). Appearance-Related Communication and Body Image Outcomes: Fat

Talk and Old Talk Among Mothers and Daughters. *Journal of Family Communication, 16*(2), 95-110.

4. Vered, S. and Walter, O. (2015) Mother-Daughter Relationship and Daughter's Body Image. *Health*, 7, 547-559.

5. Usmiani, S., & Daniluk, J. (1997). Mothers and Their Adolescent Daughters: Relationship Between Self-Esteem, Gender Role Identity, Body Image. *Journal of Youth and Adolescence, 26*(1), 45-62.

6. Lemaine, V., Cayci, C., Simmons, P.S., & Petty, P. (2013). Gynecomastia in Adolescent Males. *Seminars in Plastic Surgery*, 27(1), 56-61.

7. Puhl, R., Peterson, J., & Luedicke, J. (2013). Weight-Based Victimization: Bullying Experiences of Weight Loss Treatment-Seeking Youth. *Pediatrics, 131*(1).

8. Laderer, A. (2017, October 6). 5 Ways To Improve Your Body Image, Confidence, and Mental Health. Retrieved from talkspace.com

9. Warrell, M. (2015, February 26). Use It Or Lose It: The Science Behind Self-Confidence. Retrieved from Forbes.com

Chapter 8

1. Rodgers, Rachel & Chabrol, Henri. (2009). Parental Attitudes, Body Image Disturbance and Disordered Eating Amongst Adolescents and Young Adults: A Review. European eating disorders review: the journal of the Eating Disorders Association. 17. 137-51. 10.1002/erv.907.

Chapter 9

1. Eanes, R. Healing the Parent-Child Relationship in 6 Steps. Retrieved from creativechild.com

2. Repairing the Parent-Child Relationship. (2002, August 3). Retrieved from thesuccessfulparent.com

3. Brandt, A. (2018, May 1). Repairing Your Relationship With Your Mother. Retrieved from psychologytoday.com

Chapter 10

1. Moore, M., Jackson, E., & Tschannen-Moran, B. (2016). *Coaching Psychology Manual* (2nd ed.). New York, NY: Wolters Kluwer.

2. Christakis, N.A., & Fowler, J.H. (2007). The Spread of Obesity in a *Large* Social Network over 32 Years. *The New England Journal of Medicine.* 337, 370-379.

Made in the USA
Middletown, DE
29 January 2019